D1505858

JAN   2011

AMAZING WORKING DOGS with AMERICAN HUMANE

Protecting Children & Animals Since 1877

THERAPY DOG HEROES

Titles in the Amazing Working Dogs with American Humane Series

FIRE DOG HEROES
ISBN-13: 978-0-7660-3202-6

GUIDE DOG HEROES
ISBN-13: 978-0-7660-3198-2

POLICE DOG HEROES
ISBN-13: 978-0-7660-3197-5

SEARCH AND RESCUE DOG HEROES
ISBN-13: 978-0-7660-3201-9

SERVICE DOG HEROES
ISBN-13: 978-0-7660-3199-9

THERAPY DOG HEROES
ISBN-13: 978-0-7660-3200-2

AMAZING WORKING DOGS with

AMERICAN HUMANE

Protecting Children & Animals Since 1877

THERAPY DOG HEROES

Linda Bozzo

Bailey Books
an imprint of
Enslow Publishers, Inc.
40 Industrial Road
Box 398
Berkeley Heights, NJ 07922
USA
http://www.enslow.com

*This book is dedicated to Shira and Melanie Kirsch and their dog Tuxedo
who graciously opened their home and shared their experiences with me.*

Founded in 1877, the American Humane Association is the only national organization dedicated to protecting both children and animals. Through a network of child and animal protection agencies and individuals, American Humane develops policies, legislation, curricula, and training programs—and takes action—to protect children and animals from abuse, neglect, and exploitation. To learn how you can support American Humane's vision of a nation where no child or animal will ever be a victim of abuse or neglect, visit www.americanhumane.org, phone (303) 792-9900, or write to the American Humane Association at 63 Inverness Drive East, Englewood, Colorado, 80112-5117.

AMERICAN HUMANE

Protecting Children & Animals Since 1877

Bailey Books, an imprint of Enslow Publishers, Inc.

Copyright © 2011 by Enslow Publishers, Inc.

All rights reserved.

No part of this book may be reproduced by any means without the written permission of the publisher.

Library of Congress Cataloging-in-Publication Data

Bozzo, Linda.

    Therapy dog heroes / Linda Bozzo.

        p. cm. — (Amazing working dogs with american humane)

    Includes bibliographical references and index.

    Summary: "The text opens with a true story of a therapy dog, and then it explains the history of the therapy dog and the training methods used to transform an ordinary dog into a canine hero"—Provided by publisher.

    ISBN-13: 978-0-7660-3200-2

    ISBN-10: 0-7660-3200-0

    1. Dogs—Therapeutic use—Juvenile literature. I. Title.

    RM931.D63B69 2010

    615.8'5158—dc22   2008048020

Printed in China

052010 Leo Paper Group, Heshan City, Guangdong, China.

10 9 8 7 6 5 4 3 2 1

To Our Readers: We have done our best to make sure all Internet Addresses in this book were active and appropriate when we went to press. However, the author and the publisher have no control over and assume no liability for the material available on those Internet sites or on other Web sites they may link to. Any comments or suggestions can be sent by e-mail to comments@enslow.com or to the address on the back cover.

Every effort has been made to locate all copyright holders of material used in this book. If any errors or omissions have occurred, corrections will be made in future editions of this book.

Illustration Credits: Associated Press, pp. 16, 18; Rosemary Bennett/National Capital Therapy Dogs, Inc., p. 30; Linda Bozzo, pp. 6, 8, 11, 13, 42; Mark Cohen/National Capital Therapy Dogs, Inc., pp. 24, 26, 27; Getty Images, pp. 1, 3, 35, 44; © 2009 Jupiterimages, pp. 15, 21 (bottom); © Viktor Korotayev/Reuters/Corbis, p. 38; Shutterstock, pp. 21 (top 2), 33, 40.

Cover Illustration: Linda Bozzo.

Contents

Thank You

Enslow Publishers, Inc. wishes to thank Steve Reiman, Founder & President, Therapy Dogs of Vermont for reviewing this book.

The author would like to thank Amy Schneider who welcomed her into a local assisted-living facility so she could experience, first hand, the joy therapy dogs bring to the people they visit.

Tuxedo:
A True Story

Therapy dogs are special. They provide many great services to people. Therapy dogs bring positive changes by visiting people.

Fourteen-year-old Melanie thought her dog, Tuxedo, would make a good therapy dog. She knew Tuxedo was special. The four-year-old Portuguese water dog was very friendly and playful. He was good at following directions and loved being around people. Melanie's mom agreed.

Melanie and her dog Tuxedo

But first, Tuxedo had to be trained to see if he would make a good therapy dog. So Melanie and her mom brought Tuxedo to special classes. "Training is very important," Melanie says. "Tuxedo needed to learn to behave around groups of people. He needed to learn to work with other therapy dogs."

Therapy dogs often visit assisted-living centers or hospitals. So Tuxedo needed to be comfortable around certain types of equipment like wheelchairs and crutches. During training, Tuxedo needed to learn some basic commands like "leave it" or "sit." Melanie and her mom needed to recognize signs of Tuxedo being stressed. They watched Tuxedo, especially his face, to see if anything made him uncomfortable or upset him.

Tuxedo seemed to enjoy the time spent preparing for therapy work. After eight weeks of training and practicing, Melanie and her mom agreed that therapy work seemed to suit Tuxedo. They felt he had the skills he needed to be a therapy dog. Now it was time for them to take their tests so they could work as a team. When they passed their tests with flying colors, Melanie and her mom were thrilled! Finally, Tuxedo would begin his career in therapy work.

Together, as a team, they kept practicing their work at home. Melanie and her mom continued to bring Tuxedo to public places until they felt Tuxedo was ready to take the next step.

Melanie brought Tuxedo for a visit to her mom's office. Melanie's mom works for a speech therapy practice where people go to improve their speech.

Melanie strapped on Tuxedo's working vest. She fastened his leash. At the office, Melanie's mom used Tuxedo as a way to encourage one of her patients to speak. They began with a very simple task. Melanie's mom asked the patient to speak command words like

Melanie and Tuxedo visit a senior citizen assisted-living center.

"sit" and "stay." Having Tuxedo there urged the patient to put words together, which he was not able to do before. "I had a great time watching the patient speak to Tuxedo and give him a treat," Melanie recalled. "It was very rewarding, to see Tuxedo working with a person with disabilities."

When Tuxedo was ready, they also visited senior citizens at an assisted-living center in their community. When Melanie and her mom arrived with Tuxedo, they were greeted in the lobby by the director.

"Welcome, Tuxedo." She let them know who did and did not like dogs.

Many of the people were in wheelchairs. Others needed canes or walkers to get around. They seemed to be anxiously waiting for Tuxedo's visit.

"Would you like to pet my dog?" Melanie asked a group of women.

"Yes," one woman told her. Melanie brought Tuxedo closer. The woman reached down and stroked Tuxedo's soft fur. Tuxedo wagged his tail. Each person waited patiently for his or her turn to pet the dog.

The people at the center enjoy their time with Tuxedo.

Another woman snuggled close. At the other end of the leash, Melanie listened while people told stories about dogs they used to own. Smiles lit up their faces.

"Good dog," one woman told Tuxedo. "You are a handsome dog," added another. The woman reached over and patted Tuxedo on the head with a kind touch.

Tuxedo seemed to love all the attention. The people at the center loved Tuxedo's company.

On warm days, some of the people enjoyed a walk outside in the courtyard with Tuxedo. Just being around him made people feel better.

Therapy dogs are special. Tuxedo helps people in his community to feel special, too.

Chapter 1

The History of Therapy Dogs

Throughout history, dogs have worked with people. Early on, dogs went with men during times of war. Farmers used them to herd sheep. In 1860, nurse Florence Nightingale saw how small pets were often excellent company for the sick. Today, guide dogs work with people who are blind. Search and rescue dogs work alongside

Florence Nightingale saw that small pets were good company for sick people.

law enforcement to find lost or missing people. But therapy dogs perform a much different job. They visit people in need.

In the United States, a visiting animal program began in 1919 at St. Elizabeths Hospital in Washington, D.C. Dogs were used to work alongside patients in the hospital's mental health program.

Dogs are also used as search and rescue dogs. This dog is training to rescue a person in water.

During the 1960s, Dr. Boris Levinson was able to make progress with a patient when using his own dog, Jingles. Once Dr. Levinson began writing about the positive effects of using his dog with other patients, the idea began to grow. Soon, community programs that brought people and animals together for companionship and therapy began and continued to grow. Most of the volunteers worked with their family dogs.

Elaine Smith was a nurse. While working in England, she witnessed the benefits pets gave to her patients. When she returned to the United States, she continued to use therapy animals in health care. In 1976, Smith founded her own therapy dog organization.

Shortly after, national organizations were formed. The number of volunteers and memberships increased. People began to look more closely at how animals could change the lives of other people as well.

There was a time when most nursing homes would not allow animals to visit. That has changed, thanks to published research about the benefits of therapy dogs.

Therapy dogs can help many people!

Today, many of these same nursing homes welcome animal therapy programs.

In addition, therapy dog programs are no longer limited to hospitals to heal the sick or nursing homes to provide company to the lonely. Services provided have expanded to other areas. They help children improve their reading skills. They help heal injured people.

There is no doubt that therapy dogs make a difference. Dogs make people feel special. In some cases, they help people forget their pain. There is no therapy quite like the love of a dog.

Chapter 2

Therapy Dog Breeds

Therapy dogs can be any breed. Some popular choices are retrievers, Newfoundlands, greyhounds, and collies. Mixed breeds are also excellent choices. Regardless of the breed, a therapy dog should be calm, gentle, and especially friendly.

Dogs come in many shapes and sizes. Large dogs are good choices for some people. A large dog, like a collie, is the perfect size for people in wheelchairs to pet.

Mixed Breed

Maltese

Border Collie

21

Small dogs are also a good choice, but small dogs are easily hurt. They should only work around people who are able to treat them gently. A small breed, like a Maltese, is perfect for sitting in the lap of a child. The handler, the person handling the dog, should feel comfortable with his or her dog, no matter the size.

The dog's personality traits are more important than the dog's breed or where the dog comes from. Many wonderful therapy dogs of various breeds have been adopted from shelters and rescue groups. Both male and female dogs make good therapy dogs.

Therapy dogs and their handlers work together as a team. It is best to be sure the dog suits the handler and the type of therapy work they plan on doing.

Chapter 3

Therapy Dog Training

Before dogs perform therapy work, they must be properly socialized and trained. It is best that a dog be at least one year old before he is trained for therapy work. It is important that the dog has lived long enough with his owner to have formed a good bond. All dogs should be examined by a veterinarian. The veterinarian will make sure the dog is in good health and is up to date on vaccinations.

Therapy dogs go through training to make sure they are calm and patient.

Training classes are led by dog trainers. It is important to choose a trainer who uses gentle, positive methods. Choose someone who does not punish the dog for doing something wrong, but praises the dog for doing things right. Evaluators have experience with animals and in doing therapy work. They assess the handler-animal team for their skills and ability to do therapy work. The trainer and evaluator can instruct the handler how to prepare his or her dog for visiting programs.

Therapy dogs and their handlers train as a team. Many therapy dog teams choose to join a group when it comes to training. Guidelines may vary from group to group, but the goal is the same. It is to prepare the therapy dog team for safe and successful visits.

A therapy dog is taught to listen. The dog will learn some simple commands. Commands may include "sit," "stay," "down," and "leave it." For example, a handler might command the dog to "leave it" when a patient's medicine has fallen on the floor. A therapy dog will also learn to work around other dogs who may be visiting at the same time, without having trouble paying attention. Therapy dogs must be well behaved and know that when they are working, it is not the time to play with other dogs. Many of the people they visit use medical equipment like canes, wheelchairs, or walkers. Other medical equipment, such as machines, can make noises. A therapy dog needs to learn to be comfortable or not to be scared around loud noises.

Food is a popular reward when training dogs. Praise, playtime, and petting can also be successful training tools.

When not in class, therapy dogs continue to train at home with their handlers. They may also visit places like outdoor malls or

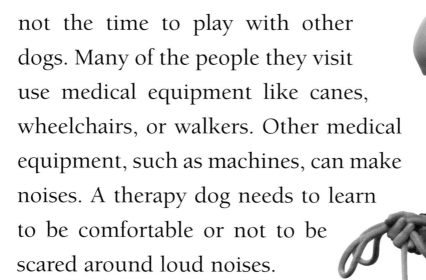

The dogs learn to obey certain commands, like "sit."

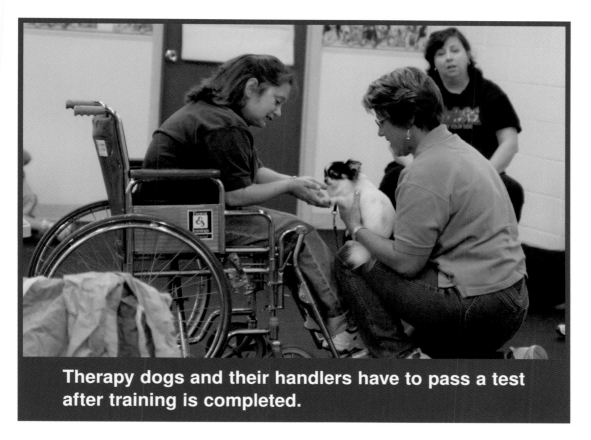

Therapy dogs and their handlers have to pass a test after training is completed.

playgrounds to practice being around people. The dog and handler will have to pass several tests in order to become a pet therapy team. In most cases, a dog will be tested on how well he listens to commands. The instructor will see how well the dog behaves with and without other dogs around. It is especially important to test therapy dogs on how well they act around medical equipment.

The amount of time it takes to train a therapy dog depends on the dog. Some dogs learn faster than others. There is no rush. The dog can be tested whenever she is ready. Some groups require that the dogs are retested throughout their working career. Whether or not they are retested, therapy dogs should continue to train as long as they continue to make visits. After the therapy dog team passes their tests, they are ready to go to work bringing joy to people in need.

Chapter 4

Therapy Dogs on the Job

Therapy dogs spend their time visiting people and sharing their love. The settings in which therapy dogs visit can vary. These dogs visit places like nursing homes, hospitals, schools, and wherever else they are needed. No matter where they visit, the therapy dog's job is always the same—to help people.

A dog should be clean and well-groomed when visiting. This includes a bath, nail trimming, and

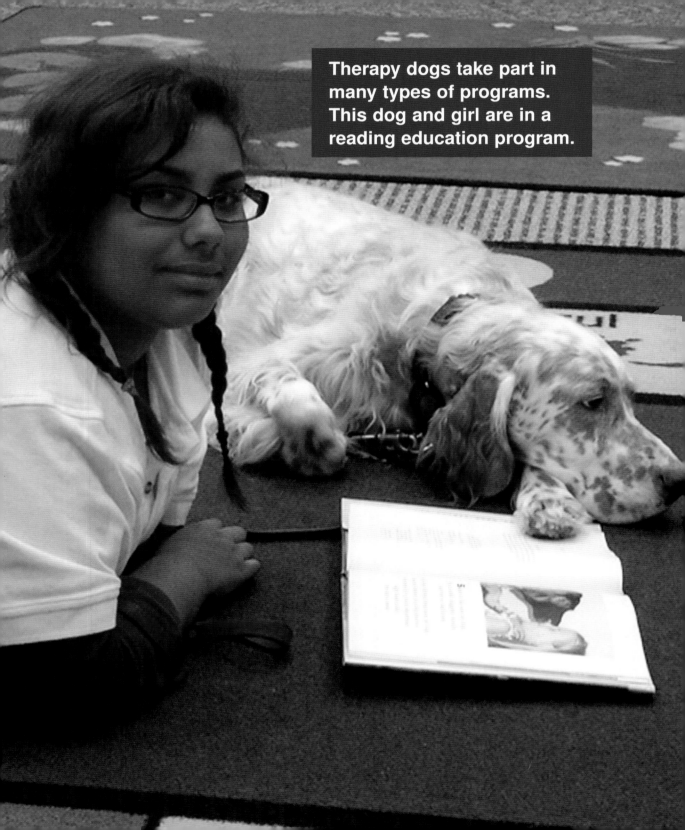

Therapy dogs take part in many types of programs. This dog and girl are in a reading education program.

thorough brushing. During visits, the therapy dog wears a collar with a tag for identification. A special therapy dog vest or bandana may also be worn. This is so everyone knows that he is a working therapy dog. It also signals to the dog that he is on the job.

When at work, the handler will keep the dog on a leash to have full control of the dog. Once the dog is prepared, it is time to visit old friends and make new ones.

A therapy dog's visit to the hospital may help people feel better by simply enjoying the dog's company. The wagging tail or wet nose of a dog can bring a smile to someone's face. A visit to a school may help a child struggling to read. Dogs are great listeners. Children love to snuggle up and read to them. Even a visit to someone who needs physical therapy can encourage a person to perform exercises that they might not do for a therapist. No matter what the setting, therapy dogs bring joy and comfort to people in need.

Upon entering the facility being visited, the dog and handler will check in with a staff person. This person instructs the handler with guidelines for their visit. The staff person may direct the handler toward people who especially like dogs and away from those who may not.

For many people, a visiting dog is an event they look forward to. Amy Schneider is the activities director at an assisted-living center for seniors. "We have a group of therapy dogs visit once a month. There are residents who choose not to participate in other activities but ask me to let them know when the therapy dogs are coming."

Some visits may be with just one dog and his handler. Other visits may include a group of dogs. During a visit, the handler introduces his or her dog

Some dogs and their handlers go to hospitals to cheer up patients.

to a person or a group of people. The therapy dog's job begins. When the handler is introduced, he or she may ask people if they would like to pet the dog. When someone says "yes," the therapy dog enjoys being petted and hugged. Many people talk about pets they used to own. Schneider truly believes animals have a special way of communicating with people. "It is a thrill to watch these animals put smiles on people's faces, especially the ones that do not have family to visit them."

In some settings, the therapy dog may need to be positioned in a way to make it easy for the person to touch the dog. "Touch can make a world of difference," Schneider says. "I've seen people's eyes light up when given the chance to touch a dog."

A small dog can sit on a towel or pad on someone's lap. The towel or pad prevents the dog's hair from getting on the person's clothing. It is also used as a signal to the dog that it is okay to visit with this person. The dog can be positioned on a small table with the handler beside to make the dog easier for the person to reach. A dog should never be left alone on a table. The dog could fall or jump off and get hurt. A large dog could be placed alongside or in front of a seated person. Large dogs may hurt a patient if they accidentally jump or lay on them in bed. That is why it is safer that the person sits on the side of the bed or on a chair to visit with the therapy dog. There are many

Dogs can help calm children and adults.

ways to position a dog so both the dog and the person are comfortable.

Visiting can be fun but it can also be stressful for a dog. After all, the dog is working. For this reason, visits should be kept to a reasonable length of time. The length of time varies from dog to dog depending on their experience and the setting they are visiting in. Handlers must always be watching out for their therapy dog. A therapy dog trusts her handler to protect her from harm and to know when a visit must end because the dog is tired or is not comfortable in the situation. "I usually recommend short visits," Schneider says. Visits should end on a positive note while the dog is still enjoying it.

Although a therapy dog's day at work draws to a close, the love these animals give to the people they visit is never ending.

Chapter 5

When Therapy Dogs Retire

Like other working dogs, there comes a time when a therapy dog retires, or no longer works. Some dogs need to retire due to old age or health problems. Some dogs retire because either they or their handlers no longer enjoy the work. It is often hard to retire a therapy dog, but what is best for the dog comes first.

Therapy dogs can make people smile.

When therapy dogs finish their working careers, they have much to look forward to. For years, they have probably brought joy to many people. These dogs enjoy retirement by continuing to share joy at home with their owners. It is important to retire a working dog a little at a time. This can be done by visiting less and for shorter periods of time. This is better than stopping suddenly. A dog may miss his job and become sad.

Most people would agree that retiring is the reward of a lifetime for both the dogs and their handlers.

After a therapy dog retires, the dog continues to live with his or her owner.

Chapter 6

Therapy Dogs Are Heroes

Heroes pass into people's lives to make a difference. Therapy dogs are heroes. Whether they are visiting the elderly or the young, they help turn frowns into smiles. At home, these dogs are loyal pets. At work, pet therapy teams volunteer their time to help people in communities everywhere. With hard work and a lot of love, they accomplish what needs to be done. These patient, people-loving dogs offer love and affection. They are

Therapy dogs can make people happy!

best known for bringing joy, comfort, and healing to the people they visit.

No one can argue the powerful connection that exists between animals and people. The effects dogs have on people are magic. That is why therapy dogs are heroes that in a small way make a big difference in our world.

Therapy dogs are truly heroes.

Glossary

breed—A certain type of dog.

evaluators—People who test visiting teams.

injured—Hurt.

therapy—Treatment of the mind or body.

therapist—A person trained in methods of treatment of the mind or body.

trait—A quality that makes one dog different from another.

vaccinations—Shots that a dog needs to protect against illness.

veterinarian—A doctor who takes care of animals.

Further Reading

Goldish, Meish. *Dogs*. New York: Bearport Pub., 2007.

Jackson, Donna M. *Hero Dogs: Courageous Canines in Action*. New York: Little, Brown, 2003.

O'Sullivan, Robyn. *More Than Man's Best Friend: The Story of Working Dogs*. Washington, D.C.: National Geographic, 2006.

Internet Addresses

American Humane Association,
  Animal-Assisted Therapy Program
  <http://www.americanhumane.org/aat>

Therapy Dogs of Vermont
  <http://www.therapydogs.org>

Index